Ely:

An experimental dream-poem

Ely:
An experimental dream-poem

PETER APPLETON

CP

THE CHOIR PRESS

First published in the United Kingdom in 2021 by
The Choir Press

ISBN 978-1-78963-189-0

To my loving family
Hilary, Cath, Ed, Jen, Andy, Beth, Caleb, Beatrice

Contents

Peter grew up in the North of England. He attended Durham University, living for his first year just down the road from Durham Cathedral. He trained in clinical psychology at Glasgow University, and has a PhD from Liverpool University.

He and his wife lived in North Wales for twenty years, where their children grew up. Peter and Hilary now live in Suffolk, close to the Fens and the Brecks.

Peter has taught at Bangor and Cambridge Universities, and worked in the NHS for many years as a children's clinical psychologist. He now has a visiting fellowship at Essex University, where his research interest is in how best to support young adults in transition from foster care and residential care.

He has been writing poetry for a few years now, with a publication in Envoi. Ely is his first long poem.

Ely:
An experimental dream-poem

———◀◦▶———

God turne us every dreme to good!

Geoffrey Chaucer, *The House of Fame*, c. 1380

PART 1

Up, up and away

_____

1
That golden day I had known we were ready;
more than anything else I wanted to go.

2
On one fine East Anglian day
  she upped and went,
    no fanfare, no gathering of medieval masons
    to wish her well.

Part ship, part starship,
  she left her moorings and sailed
    over the railways,
      over Silicon Fen,
        over Westminster, and the Tower.

A bit Old Testament,
  we wondered if she might be on course
    for the Middle East.

Or would she sail to Rome
  and park up, smiling, outside St Peter's?

With her raw Norman sides she looked unlikely
     for space travel, but her
          Octagon shone, and
no doubt she was ahead of us.
Aircraft sent up just to look
     remarked on a sort of perfection,
          no crumbling or shaking.

Over the Sargasso Sea she rested
     and again over West Mariana on a dark new moon
     night,

then to Antarctica.

3

Why do dreams mix time, language, place, people,
bishops, everything a muddle? I dream of fens. I also
dream of the vast forests that used to clothe warm
'Antarctica'. And my dreams are of the prairies of
South America. I dream of the sea, and of the travels
of eels, ウナギ.

   I dream in our own fen language, of eaus and flus,
leams and lodes and hythes. I dream of Queen Adelaide,
Lark Bank at Prickwillow, Shippea Hill, Eriswell St
Laurence and St Peter, then Brecks and more larks.

   And yet more fen, at March, Manea, and Lynn,
          Wicken and Reach.
And I dream of Antarctic ice floes, leads, lines, and
lanes.

   I dream of Frank Hurley, the handsome, courageous
Australian photographer on Shackleton's *Endurance*

expedition: a photo of bearded Frank in his twenties, and another photograph of him high up in the *Endurance* rigging, 'on the extreme end of the top gallant-yard, to get panoramic views of the Pack', or precariously (he wouldn't say so) perched on the end of the ship's bowsprit, camera pointed down, filming the ice being cut, rammed, ever so gently.

But Antarctica is a continent.

Eels move out of willow slips in Popham's Eau, swim to Ouse, and out to sea.

4
She could read my mind
like the eagle who carries Geoffrey up into the heavens.
> But he that bare me gan espye
> That I so thought.

And I was in her mind.
> God turne us every dreme to goode!

In South America we had discovered a great warm-blooded creature with octagonal heart-brain, self-heal, and quiet flight. It lived in glades, among strange trees and ferns from a forgotten time, near to open grasslands. Deep dark brown, like earth, its plumage breathed and watched and heard.

As we walked out onto the La Plata plain, endless flocks of chajás called. In the evening the entire multitude of birds covering the marsh for miles around burst forth into a tremendous evening song. It was as if half a million voices broke out on a dark lonely plain. In this mighty noise, which sounded louder than the sea thundering on a rocky coast, I seemed to be able to distinguish hundreds, even thousands, of individual voices. The chajás, like the skylark, love to soar upwards when singing, and at such times when they have risen till their dark bulky bodies appear like floating specks on the blue sky, or until they disappear from sight altogether, the notes become wonderfully etherealised by distance to a soft silvery sound. It seems strange that so ponderous a fowl with only six feet and a half spread of wings should possess a power of soaring equal to that of vultures and eagles. In bright warm weather, in winter and spring, it spends a great part of the day in the upper regions of the air. It sings while soaring, seeming to exult in its sublime power and freedom.

5

As if she had stem cells, our northwest transept, lost sometime in the fifteenth century, has regrown. And, in regrowing, has formed a conservatory, with trees, flowers, ferns – our own botanical transept. Our plants are from the Anthropocene going back to the Cretaceous, including our own *Nothofagus antarctica*. We also have some friendly Japanese maples, 紅葉, five of them low-spreading and angelic, near the west end of the north aisle.

Our upper galleries (previously called triforia or tribunes) have become open, light, nautical, look-out, look-in, all-around.

The warm Octagon Lantern 'time/space engyn' has a resting state of complete silence, but regularly we hear an extended series of 'calls' or 'chuckles', which sound like a busy group of fieldfares in an English winter. We find ourselves looking high up into the Lantern, but we don't see anything. Oddly, most of us sense that the chuckling means the engyn is dreaming. Our resident Cambridge neuroscientist found herself saying, 'Lots of REM, like a newborn baby.'

And we, with a smile, dream of Edward III's master carpenter William Hurley, who in the fourteenth century designed the vast oaken expressive palm branches wooden vault, housing Alan de Walsingham's great Octagon, all now our powerhouse of mortal energy.

6

No more railway   no more AK-47   no more A10
   no more heavy farm artic   no more rumble
   no more cuts
no more mobile   no more cellphone   no more
   smartphone
no more Radio 4   no more corporate   no more fame
   no more cuts

7

In our own fenland Roman Stonea, buying meat and fish.

   People in the streets smiling, arm-in-arm or holding
   hands.

Would sister Winchester go next?

Would Narbonne leave its étangs and fly with flamingos?

Would Amiens, with its arc-boutants, take wing?

Eels by lesch, through leach, past gatherings of glaives.
Lines and leads, in the ice, on the sea.

PART 2
Domestic

1

Our wonderful Octagon guide, John Landymore, had been on the roof with a small tour when our mother-church had taken it into her head to sally forth into the heavens. Good East Anglian that he is, he guided his seven charges back through the roof door and down the top stairs into the massive internal elevated oaken Octagon/Lantern frame. He reported that there was a bit of turbulence, and one of the tour mentioned health and safety, but all was well, and they saw from inside and first-hand the Octagon super-charging its time-space engyn. Throughout he stayed calm, and saw the party down all the narrow medieval stairs. The party included three ladies from Gdańsk, who were saying how much they loved England, and Ely in particular.

2

We have a cat, a ship's cat – he was found next to the Gurney stove just outside Bishop Nicholas West's Chantry Chapel (where he has an ancient cushioned chair). We christened him Mrs Chippy. He enjoys walking around the high gallery rail.

We realised, after a little research, that Mrs Chippy knew which side his bread was buttered on. Bishop West, who was Bishop of Ely from 1515 to 1534, had 'lived in the greatest splendour of any Prelate in his time' (he had been a brilliant diplomat for Henry VIII, and was 'rewarded' with the Ely bishopric). He was also a kind man, 'feeding warm meat and drink to the excess of 200 people per day'. He was also a learned man, although as an undergraduate he had 'had a reputation as a troublemaker'. We smiled as we read what he had inscribed on the walls of his chapel: *Gratia Dei sum id quod sum* ('By the grace of God I am what I am', 1 Corinthians 15:10).

3

Fugue – out. Our sub-organist is excelling with humour – his own arrangements of big 'atmospheric' pieces – yesterday Debussy's/arr. Leopold Stokowski's 'La cathédrale engloutie', and today John Adams's 'Short Ride in a Fast Machine'. On other days a different big: Mingus's 'Better Git It in Your Soul', followed by 'E's Flat Ah's Flat Too'. On a particularly cold day, beginning to transcribe Frederick Delius's 'Summer Night on the River'.

4

Our mobiles were and are mercifully moribund. On our
first day we performed hilariously a little dramatic play
in Bishop West's Chantry Chapel, re-enacting, with all
our dead phones, the Monty Python's Flying Circus
words:
The plumage don't enter into it
      it's   stone   dead
  this parrot is no more
    it has ceased to be
      it's expired and gone to meet its maker
        this is a late parrot
         it's a stiff
           bereft of life
             it rests in peace.
If you hadn't nailed it to the perch, it would be pushing
up daisies.
It's rung down the curtain and joined the choir invisible.
This   is   an   ex-parrot.

5

And so to bed
      we sleep comfortably in two deep dormitories
        which have grown long
           where a crypt might have been
           unagi no nedoko
           utterly dark in Antarctic summer.

6

I have Abbess Etheldreda continuously in mind, as if the
seventh century is now.

PART 3
Geography

1

Perhaps not many people know about the English fens, near Ely and Cambridge and Lincoln and Brandon and Peterborough: the prehistory of human settlement on fen edges and 'islands'; bronze age droves, ferries, causeways, barrows; an iron age fort followed by an important Roman fenland town at Stonea; in medieval times rich summer pastures, winter flooding, and hundreds of small human communities; the 'paradox' of peat contraction (and surface wasting) after massive straight fen cuts and drainage in the seventeenth century, leaving new waterways higher than the land they were draining, and angry Fenland men and women. Hundreds of windmills for water, moving water, some of the time. Then hybrid steam engines to pump water, some of the time. Rich rich rich Fenland agricultural land supplying much of England's veg. The forever open skies beauty of the place.

2

We were helpless intruders in a strange world.
Ernest Shackleton, *South*, London: Penguin,
2002, p.71

I had been dreaming about Ernest Shackleton's *South*, chapter IV, 'Loss of the *Endurance*', a dream I think provoked by the small schematic drawing (by Shackleton himself?), as if from above, of the ship surrounded by pressure ridges of ice, pools of 'young ice', and the stark word *FLOE* written, in capitals, in each of four directions.

3

Our   prayers   are
         in   air
         bare   and   pleyne
  as   our   era

Our   hymns
        in   eyre   y-broken.

PART 4

What is she doing?

———

1

Our cathedral wasn't exactly prolixe; didn't have a
superfluite of *words*.

At first, as she took us close to the Transantarctic
Mountains, TAM, I wondered if she thought TAM meant
something to do with transcendental meditation,
     but she was too restless, footloose, for that.

Then I began to think she wanted to have a ball
     with the wild electromagnetism of the Pole and the
     TAM

     after Pacific seamounts
     waiting for a coronal mass ejection

     on her own sunset strip,
     her own Rammstein moments, 'Mutter', or 'Feuer
frei'.

After 900 years of a life sédentaire in the fens, might she
need
     Beardmore and Nimrod,
     orogeny, flux, geochronology
     and a full tectonic?

O God, thought I, *that madest kynde –*
shal I no other weyes dye?
Will Joves me stellefye?
Or what thinge may this sygnifye?

Geochronology, and some geomagnetism, she did want,
as did Japanese eels, *Anguilla japonica*, as they found
their spawning grounds of West Mariana.

2
Now kythe thyn engyne and myght!
    not dombe as any stoon.

Much had happened during her short life: her Norman
tower falling, the attacks on the body and face of her
Lady Chapel – and the mutilations of Bishop West's
chapel, her congregatiounes dwindling now, those two
nice men burnt at the stake in 1555, and so on. And all
around her, the destruction of the ancient fenland – what
did Bishop John Morton think he was doing when he
made one of the first cuts? – and it was a big one – and
he went on to be Archbish of Canterbury – *and* Lord
Chancellor!

But it is a short life; she relishes her dreams of warm
Antarctica, of being truly close to India, Australia, New
Zealand, South Africa, Patagonia, and Amazonia.

She is pleased her Lady Chapel has great independence of spirit, has brought all those nice people back
from Rome, that all her art has been renewed.

She has now found Archean grey gneisses.

While she was being Archean and Precambrian, I read Job.

Where were you when I laid the foundation of the earth?

Tell me, if you have understanding.

Who determined its measurements – surely you know?

Or who stretched the line upon it?

On what were its bases sunk,

or who laid its cornerstone

when the morning stars sang together

and all the heavenly beings shouted for joy?

3
shortly before our return

      in our dormitories
      unagi no nedoko

      the strangest dream

stamping from above
      in the old nave

  I all ice under
         a subglacial lake

  understanding frozen.

PART 5

*Joys of the
Lady Chapel*

Our Lady Chapel
    the physics escapes me
    when galley provisions were low
    would pop to Hobart.

With a few of our youngsters on board
    she'd collect groceries, our post
    and more.

Might she travel first to the alluvial Indo-Gangetic
plains, where she had temple friends?

No, via Rome,
    not, as it happens, to pick up
    wild culinary treats, or watch
    ragazzi on scooters, or swifts in the evening sky.

No, in Rome all her medieval stained glass was restored
    in greens and golds, and more:
    her fabulous sculptures, lost during the Reformation,
    were renewed, as in a dream.

Inside and out, brackets and canopies waiting,
    full again with Mary's story,
    147 their number   empty niches or broken faces
    restored   returned
    in their nodding   sensuous   double-curved   3D
    ogee   ogive   cusped   gabled   crocketed
    absolute Christian joy.
And Mr Pevsner stopped being sad.

(Although in Rome she had insisted that a few
twentieth-century poets should be added during the
sculpture renewal: Allen G and his dear mother Naomi,
Denise L and her dear sister Olga. They sat high up,
where old bishops had previously perched.)

On the way back from the Holy City, being young,
and all on board,
    she gave some cheek to
    a lumbering but beautiful RAAF C-17 Globemaster,
    stuffed with snowcats,
    en route to Wilkins, or McMurdo Sound.

She streamed ahead, all green and flowing Dec, and,
steadying herself, naughtily flashed polar sunlight from
    her fabulously restored stained glass,
    sledging the Aussie pilots.

Why, then
    off she'd go, our little Gothic starship,
    nothing medieval about her.

On board, waifs, strays, resident fellows, lady rabbis, beats, deacons, Denise, imams, and more.
What would Mother say?

While her Lady Chapel had been away, our mother-church had tilted, slightly 'down' in the 'south', moderately 'up' to the 'north'. Now, equilibrium restored, she seemed, as far as we could tell, pleased to have new friends.

Part 6

It is no litel thing

It is no litel thinge a man to dwelle in monasteries and congregacions.

Thomas à Kempis, *Imitation of Christ*, c. 1420

Some of our flock had decided that the monastic life was not for them and had sent an ambassador to request 'a transfer to earth'. Could she please drop them off somewhere, anywhere, on land, and preferably in 'not too cold a place'? Well, she had a few fieldfare days and nights, and then began gently to move toward South America. When we looked down, we beheld feldes and playnes, and now hilles and now montaynes, now valeys, now forestes.

After circling over Patagonia, she eventually came down in felds and playnes near La Plata, just south of Buenos Aires. We all said our goodbyes, and the little band walked off through the Galilee, and out onto the steppe, with their city in view.

She rested for a while, then away we went, back to our new home, between heaven, earth, sky, and sea.

PART 7

Blue skies liturgy

———

It hath been the wisdom of the Church of England ever since the first compiling of her Publick Liturgy, to keep the mean between the two extremes, of too much stiffness in refusing, and of too much easiness in admitting any variation from it.

The Book of Common Prayer, 1662

Come, sit down every mother's son, and rehearse your parts.

William Shakespeare, *A Midsummer Night's Dream*, Act III, Scene I

One of our visitors sang operatic bass-baritone, and we young began to sing too.

Quite soon, he stopped us,
 saying, 'Get used to making a noise;
 do not be miniature, or English.'

He SANG Vaughan Williams's setting of 'Love
 bade me welcome. Yet my soul drew back' –
and our tears did flow.

Gradually, one of us young began again to sing, and SANG, SANG, SANG,

  singing until he tried to stop her, to say something

  but the young sang on.

  He said *you're difficult to stop.*

  'Don't stop!!!' we said.

And the young all sang, like the morning stars.

PART 8

The return of the native

———

1
Suddenly we were back

> by the River Lark at Isleham Fen. Fifty Farm, Lucky Bank,

> following the river to Lark Bank, Prickwillow,

> by all the lines of the railway through Queen Adelaide

> skirting Ely.

2
Flew in

> to a marshy place which was called Pymore

> by the nonconformist chapel

over the fields,
    Dunkirk, California,
        Bishop's Palace at Downham,
        Black Bank station,
           Engine Farm, and the remnants of
           windmills.

People pleased to see us on the horizon again

    came, visited from mid-fen tree near Whittlesey,

    took photos.

In a miracle, photographs were found to contain extras:

    a parked berg by the nave, Eocene penguins outside
    the Galilee,
    little antic fish by the Prior's Door, lovely
    leptocephali in the chapel windows,
    pink/purple skies.

Videos had extras too:

    underwater song of sub-adult leopard seal,

    and always *Anguilla*, silver.

Next door, the nonconformist chapel came back to life.

Local maps and illustrated histories had to be adjusted;
people *demanded* ecclesiastical accuracy:

huts, penguins, flying tents, Archean grey gneiss, *Anguilla japonica*, leptocephali.

3

Our galleries still light, open, like Laon.

In our Galilee, another miracle:
>   the listener heard not
>   her own language, but
>   the other's tongue,
>   understanding.

4

One morning several black SUVs were seen undulating across the fen. A door opened, and out stepped an archbishop of his time, in full regalia. He plodded across a black field to the Galilee, where flying around outside were many colourful extinct southern fauna, some mega, having their own Latitude festival. Penguins were in charge of discipline. Just about smiling, the archbishop waded through the mêlée, into the Galilee, where he heard only babble. Like Black Rod he banged several times on the cathedral door, but to no avail. There was nothing to do but retreat, and hot-foot back over the fen.

A few children had started an online anime magazine called

Fly Ely!

Encouragement to the young.

As our mother-church landed
    back in the fens,

everywhere, myriads of godly heavenly places in wood,
    canvas, a few in stone,
        took off,
            each a little light.

All together, new constellaciouns and galaxies
    in starry starry skies.

Airlines grounded all commercial flights.
    Military thought twice.

Alice by flus and eaus,
    early avian voice.

Poem notes

———⟨o⟩———

this do-it-yourself-poem kit / /
a work which seems ready to fly apart when touched, but in which also everything comes to seem connected with everything else.

AC Spearing, discussing Chaucer's *The House of Fame*, in *Medieval Dream Poetry*, Cambridge: Cambridge University Press, 1976, p. 73

Part 1: Up, up and away

1.1: Two lines from Elizabeth Bishop's poem 'Santarém', with changes.

1.2: Ely Cathedral is known as 'the ship of the Fens'. 'As one approaches Ely on foot or on a bicycle, or perhaps in an open car, the cathedral dominates the picture for miles around' (Simon Bradley & Nikolaus Pevsner, 2014, *Cambridgeshire*, London: Yale University Press, p. 484). Having 'taken off', the cathedral travels south via two global eel spawning grounds (Sargasso Sea and West Mariana).

1.2, 1.3, 1.7, and throughout: Eel lives and migration. 'Take an eel in a Danish stream – when it is time to mate, they do not choose the easy option and find an eel in the same river to breed with. Instead, they embark on a perilous 5,000 kilometre journey to spawn in the Sargasso Sea' (Kristian Sjøgren, 'Scientists solve the riddle of eel evolution', ScienceNordic, 11 August 2015). For more details of the extraordinary story (and remaining mysteries) of the evolution of eel migration, see David Righton et al., 'The Anguilla spp. migration problem: 40 million years of evolution and two millennia of speculation', *Journal of Fish Biology* 81(2), 365–386.

Japanese eels migrate to the west of the Pacific Mariana Islands, to near the West Mariana Ridge, an underwater series of seamounts (actually a 3,000 kilometre ridge of eighty-two submarine volcanic mountains, some with peaks very close to the surface of the sea, on the eastern edge of the Philippine Sea tectonic plate). As the new moon approaches, the parent eels search for a signal that only eels 'know', then start to gather and spawn; the signal could be geomagnetic, or it could be seawater-temperature-related, or perhaps turbulence (see Mari Kuroki and Katsumi Tsukamoto, *Eels on the Move: Mysterious Creatures over Millions of Years*, Hadano: Tokai University Press, 2012). Larval eels, called leptocephali ('slim head' in Greek), have flat, transparent bodies resembling willow leaves. Japanese eel leptocephali spend about four months travelling from West Mariana to find East Asian freshwater habitats, growing as they go, from very few millimetres to about sixty millimetres; they then metamorphose and enter rivers as 'elvers'. Once 'settled', they turn into relatively sedentary 'yellow eels', living in burrows or under stones, with quite small home ranges. After some years they turn into silver eels, ready for a second long sea journey, to find their spawning grounds. The biology of the incoming and outgoing migratory journeys is still poorly understood. In the East Anglian Fens, eels used to form an important part of the lives of people, and of course the local economies; glaives (1.7) were pronged spears used to catch eels.

1.3: Dreamy reflections, thinking of Geoffrey Chaucer's *House of Fame*, as well as the Fens and Antarctica. On Frank Hurley, see Caroline Alexander's brilliant book *The Endurance: Shackleton's Legendary Antarctic Expedition* (New York: Knopf, 1998), with many superbly reproduced photographs by Hurley.

1.4: Geoffrey Chaucer's *The House of Fame* in mind (eagle reading Geoffrey's mind, and vice versa), Durham Medieval and Renaissance Texts 3, Institute of Medieval and Early Modern Studies, Durham University, and Pontifical Institute of Mediaeval Studies, Toronto, 2013 (second edition), edited with an introduction, notes and glossary by Nick Havely.

1.4: 'As we walked out' para: for this section thanks entirely to WH Hudson's *The Naturalist in La Plata* (third edition), London: Chapman and Hall, 1895, chapter XVIII, 'The Crested Screamer (*Chauna chavarria*)'.

Part 2: Domestic
2.2: In her 1998 book *The Endurance*, Caroline Alexander describes how the cat Mrs Chippy – who was brought on board by carpenter Harry McNish, and who became the ship's mascot – took great delight in leaping across the kennel roofs of the sledging dogs, tantalisingly out of reach.

2.4: Thanks to canonical Monty Python parrot sketch.

2.5: *Unagi no nedoko* – Japanese metaphor describing

long and narrow domestic rooms, like eel hideaways / sleeping places / burrows, usually cosy – but perhaps not (see later in poem)?

2.6: Abbess (later Saint) Etheldreda founded Anglo-Saxon Ely Abbey in 672. She presided over a mixed community of women and men.

Part 3: Geography

3.1: Susan Oosthuizen's *The Anglo-Saxon Fenland* (Oxford: Windgather Press, 2017) provides a superb interdisciplinary history of Fenland at the time of Etheldreda. Francis Pryor's *The Fens: Discovering England's Ancient Depths* (London: Head of Zeus, 2019) is also a wonderful read, on the archaeology of the Fens.

Part 4: What *is* she doing?

4.1: The Transantarctic Mountains (TAM) constitute one of the earth's great intra-continental mountain belts, extending for more than 3,000 kilometres across the continent. Their origins go back to the late Neoproterozoic break-up of Rodinia. See David H Elliot, 'The geological and tectonic evolution of the Transantarctic Mountains: a review', Geological Society of London, Special Publications 381, 7–35, 1 July 2013.

'O God, thought I' from Chaucer's *House of Fame,* as very worried Geoffrey is taken for a ride by the wordy eagle.

4.2: Engyne / Engine: see Nick Havely's commentary on *House of Fame,* lines 523–528 (see note 1.4 for full citation). Enjoy Middle English meanings of *engine* (see online Middle English dictionary, University of

Michigan) plus modern meanings of *engine*. *Engyn*, noun, Middle English and so on: talent, ingenuity, trickery, cunning, a plot, mode or manner of construction, design, machine (for torture), machine for assaulting fortifications, or casting stones over walls, or weapons of personal combat, penis, a person regarded as another's instrument or agent, a tool, the universe, a railway locomotive, a machine for producing energy of motion from some other form of energy, esp. heat that the machine itself generates, search engine.

Warm Antarctica: 'Today Antarctica is a continent locked in ice with nearly 98% of its current terrain covered by permanent ice and snow. Yet for the vast majority of its existence the Antarctic landmass was ice-free and supported a diversity of plants and animals' (David Cantrill & Imogen Poole, *The Vegetation of Antarctica through Geological Time*, Cambridge: Cambridge University Press, 2012, p. 1).

Morton's Leam was dug in the late fifteenth century under the direction of Bishop Morton of Ely.

William Wolsey and Robert Pygot, Protestant martyrs, were burnt at the stake in Ely in 1555.

East Antarctica and close friends in early Jurassic Gondwana.

Archean grey gneiss: very, very old earthly rock. See Elliot, 2013, cited in note 4.1.

4.3: 'And stampen, as men doon aftir eles' (Chaucer, *House of Fame*, line 2154; see note 1.4 for full citation).

Part 5: Joys of the Lady Chapel

The cathedral Lady Chapel is described lyrically by Pevsner in *Cambridgeshire* (Simon Bradley & Nikolaus Pevsner, 2014, London: Yale University Press).

'Dec' is Nikolaus Pevsner's shorthand for 'Decorated', as in English Gothic architecture c. 1290–c. 1350.

Part 6: It is no litel thinge

Acknowledging Chaucer's *House of Fame* again (see note 1.4) for 'feldes and playnes – - – - – '.

The Galilee forms the spacious west porch of the cathedral.

Part 7: Blue skies liturgy

Lines from George Herbert ('Love (III)'), and Vaughan Williams's setting of Herbert: *Five Mystical Songs*.

Part 8: The return of the native

8.5: 'Poetical Physics': thank you multiple times to incredible book (now an *olde bok*) on Chaucer's *House of Fame* by JAW Bennett, *Chaucer's Book of Fame*, Oxford: Oxford University Press, 1968, chapter 2.

Early avian voice: see Patrick O'Connor's article 'Palaeontology: Ancient avian aria from Antarctica', *Nature* 538, 468–469.

Background ideas

This experimental dream-poem has several imaginative places/times it keeps going back to.

Making the cathedral religious (again)

One of the reasons she took off, perhaps, and only perhaps, was to escape the life of being 'chronically on show', and the secular life outside and sometimes in.

She is now busy beginning, and only beginning, to review some of her long history, in more religiously improvisational places, and via the freedom of dream.

She remembers that the 'islands' of the fens were, in early medieval times, places where Christian groups, and individual Christians, would go and seek silence and contemplative isolation. She is Christian, while also being open to wider religious experience and people. She wants to be openly ecumenical in the broadest sense. Being ecumenical includes her awareness of her earth-place ecology, in Fenland, and above Antarctica. She is conscious of the larger world of the universe/galaxie, and its awful bigness.

Sung song is important – the human voice; her choir and sub-organist are with her in spirit and in humour. And as she takes off maybe she has in mind Beethoven's first symphony, the second movement – 'Andante cantabile con moto' – played carefree, with youthful expectation and excitement. For instance, we might have in mind the performance of Philippe Jordan with the Wiener Symphoniker, recorded in Vienna in February 2017.

The cathedral's imaginary residentiary canon is deeply involved in the search for a more religious life for the cathedral and its people. Also dreamlike, sometimes her thoughts are picked up by her cathedral, and sometimes vice versa.

Meanwhile, the cathedral's Lady Chapel has a seriously smiley role as a young person with attitude (and won't listen to Beethoven).

The poem thinks about air, wind, fens, Pentecost, all together in one place, TAM, foreign languages, ice, and visitors from Rome.

Fenland as place

The cathedral has always been aware of her diocesan large-skies place, her Fenlands and their peculiar languages, people, water, birds, eels, cuts for drainage, the twentieth century ploughing up and destroying its own history, and the recent heavy traffic of accelerated economic rationality.

Finding Chaucer dream-poetry, and Middle English

Ely Cathedral was founded and built before Chaucer was born. But later, after the collapse of her Norman crossing in February 1322, the Octagon and Lady Chapel were built – this in the same century as Geoffrey Chaucer. His *House of Fame* (probably written in the 1380s), and his other dream poetry, have provided very important sources of ideas. The whole idea of a dream vision poem becomes possible through reading Chaucer, and through reading wonderful secondary literature on *House of Fame*. The Middle English words *swevene*, *avisioun*, *meten*, and so on, all overlapping concepts of dream, all used by Chaucer in a wonderfully chaotic and inventive way in *House of Fame*, have been wonderful to discover, connecting to the cathedral's childlike REM revision of her life for the future (but dreams don't have tenses; see Gregory Bateson, 'Metalogue: What is an instinct?' in Gregory Bateson (ed.), *Steps to an Ecology of Mind*, New York, NY: Ballantine, 1972, pp. 38–58).

The Anthropocene and the Great Acceleration

She is aware of the Anthropocene, via the peaty losses, cuts, and traffic of her homelands, but also through her own secularisation at home – her being, over hundreds of years, almost emptied of God (see Charles Taylor's 2007 book *A Secular Age*, Cambridge, MA: Harvard University Press). She wants to contribute to poetic and dream-like thinking about the Anthropocene, from particular places (her Fenland diocese, and then Antarctica, via eel spawning grounds), and a particular position (her re-finding her religious and spiritual awareness). She has her own Great Acceleration, 'I'm out of here', with some playful reversals of ideas, including *House of Fame* reversals (e.g. she doesn't travel *to* a House of Fame/Rumour; she travels, she hopes and prays, *away from* it). She is conscious of Antarctica's earthly history, and the early loss of megafauna in southern continents, and is pleased to be in southern latitudes as new megafauna.

Eels

Her name includes eels and her Fenland early history includes eels; they are now 'threatened' or 'critically endangered', like so many other species. She is conscious of their fishiness, their 'uncharismatic' existence, and wants to touch them, perhaps inspired by the way that Christ might have spoken to the 'lowliest of the low'. She is fascinated by their truly astonishing life cycle and migrations, much of which has eluded/eludes scientists. Their 'face' (see Levinas, below), and their living spaces. Her name/her 'self'.

The 1914–1917 *Endurance* Trans-Antarctic Expedition led by Ernest Shackleton

Our cathedral and her canon are deeply moved by the story of Shackleton's extraordinary human leadership in the Antarctic, and the imaginary residentiary canon would have liked to meet Frank Hurley, the expedition's 'gifted and gritty' photographer. We are all, those of us dreaming, struck by the special language (also in Shackleton's book, and in Hurley's letters) about the ship, the ice and sea and bergs and leads and floes, the seasons and the vast skies. We have the ship's cat Mrs Chippy as a guest star. The *Endurance* (like Darwin and FitzRoy's *Beagle*) had an excellent ship's library whose *bokes* Mr Chaucer would no doubt have appreciated. The word *Providence,* used by Ernest Shackleton in *South: The Endurance Expedition*, is also important to our canon: 'When I look back at those days I have no doubt that Providence guided us, not only across those snow fields, but across the storm-white sea that separated Elephant Island from our landing place on South Georgia' (*South*, London: Penguin, 2002, p. 204).

The cathedral's imaginary residentiary canon
'Canons are definitely amongst the big guns of the Church of England, although perhaps the smallest of them' (Keith Alsop, 'Canon', Church of England Companion, churchofenglandglossary.co.uk / dictionary / definition / canon, accessed August 2018).

A large part of the dream-poem is written by an imaginary young woman priest, or more accurately residentiary canon, who goes AWOL with her cathedral and may eventually become the on-board twenty-first-century abbess, like St Etheldreda, who founded the church and abbey in Ely in the Anglo-Saxon seventh century.

The cathedral is probably female (check with Mrs Chippy), and the Lady Chapel most definitely is. In a low-key way (or perhaps not low-key) the poem wants to tease the wider churches, of many faiths and denominations, for their approach to gender in the twenty-first century, and their seemingly wilful lack of recognition of women's actual, real-life leadership.

Emmanuel Levinas
In 'reaching out', the cathedral is aware of the infinite, both physically and in fellowship with all people. See Emmanuel Levinas, *Ethics and Infinity*, Pittsburgh, PA:

Duquesne University Press, 1985; *Otherwise Than Being or Beyond Essence*, Pittsburgh: Duquesne University Press, 1981.

She is aware of all the languages lost since she was built. And Pentecost, and civil wars, and internecine wars, and the dreadful wars against indigenous peoples, and she has had enough of committees and rules and laws (although she knows these must exist).

She is / not / sadly / for us / poetry writers and readers / an anarchist, but perhaps might like to be. ('Anarchists also offer a positive theory of human flourishing, based upon an ideal of non-coercive consensus building. Anarchism has inspired practical efforts at establishing utopian communities, radical and revolutionary political agendas, and various forms of direct action.' Metaphysics Research Lab, 'Anarchism', Stanford Encyclopedia of Philosophy, 2017, plato.stanford.edu/entries/anarchism, accessed November 2020).

Young

But she is young (when compared with Archean grey gneiss). As are eel leptocephali, and the teenage Lady Chapel.

Acknowledgements

The poem began life early in October 2016, when the first section was written; then a lecture – 'When Antarctica Was Green' (Cambridge, 11 October 2016) by Jane Francis, director of the British Antarctic Survey – became very important for the rest of the poem. The poem was completed in February 2020.

The library at the Scott Polar Research Institute was invaluable; thanks also to Cambridge University Library, the Whipple Library at Cambridge, and the Albert Sloman Library at Essex University.

I am deeply grateful for three detailed, thoughtful, and warm sets of comments on the draft poem (April and May 2017; October 2018).

Readings: Poetry Aloud, Bury St Edmunds (Suffolk Poetry Society); CB1, Cambridge. Thank you for great feedback.

Thanks also for inspiration from a Sea of Faith Network poetry meeting at St John's Church, Waterloo, March 2017, and a poetry workshop at the Poetry School, London, May 2017, where part of the poem was discussed.

Many thanks to Dr David Righton, behavioural ecologist at the Centre for Environment, Fisheries and Aquaculture Science, Lowestoft, for correspondence, and for sending a copy of the spectacular book by his Japanese colleagues Mari Kuroki and Katsumi Tsukamoto, Eels on the Move (see note '1.2, 1.3, 1.7, and throughout').

Many thanks to Derek Adams, Eve Bertelsen, Anne and Ian Garmston, Shota Moriue, Fay Roberts, Sheri Smith, Richard Whiting.